Another *world* is possible Another *world* is here

An Advent Course based on the Year A Readings

Valerie Flessati
Bruce Kent

kevin mayhew

First published in 2007 by

KEVIN MAYHEW LTD
Buxhall, Stowmarket, Suffolk, IP14 3BW
E-mail: info@kevinmayhew.com
www.kevinmayhew.com

Acknowledgement: The publishers wish to thank those who have given their permission to reproduce copyright material in this publication. We hope that no copyright has been infringed. If the contary be the case a correction will be made in any reprint of this book.

9 8 7 6 5 4 3 2 1

ISBN 978 1 84417 802 5
Catalogue No. 1501029

Cover design by Sara-Jane Came
Edited and typeset by Katherine Laidler

Printed and bound in Great Britain

Contents

Introduction

This short book is aimed at making the four weeks of Advent a positive period of prayer, reflection and action. If you are searching for the deeper meaning of Advent and Christmas, then join us – so are we.

This has been written for individuals but can easily be adapted for use in a parish group. Use the ideas in it for your family preparations, or invite other Christians for a simple Advent discussion and candle ceremony in your home.

The approach of Christmas gives many of us mixed feelings. Expectations can be created which are impossible to meet. We know that we ourselves, tied by our own limitations and fixed habits, are part of the problem.

We look forward to the winter holidays, having time to relax and enjoy good company with family and friends . . . but are also caught up in the tensions that can surface when we get together with our nearest and dearest.

There's the desire to understand more fully the Christian feast, the mysterious hope embodied in this baby born so long ago yet bringing us freedom here and now in the twenty-first century . . . contrasted with the emptiness of the Christmas shop-till-you-drop experience that leaves some on the edge of financial disaster.

There's the excitement of recreating for children the wonder of angels, stars, sparkling lights and presents . . . alongside our grown-up knowledge that life, with its sadness, illness and loss, is never going to be so trouble-free and innocent again.

And there's our deep longing that all God's family should live in peace, plenty, freedom and justice . . . contrasted with the reality that for so many is cruelty, war, poverty and fear, instead.

So if you too have mixed feelings at the prospect of Christmas, this book is for you. Advent is a time to 'mind the gap' between the promise of God's kingdom – the vision of harmony on God's holy mountain, lambs living peacefully with wolves, and all that that symbolises – and our disturbing, muddled, confusing and sinful world which so badly needs a Saviour today. Advent gives us hope that another world is possible, and announces that, with Jesus, another world is here.

About this book

For each of the four weeks of Advent, you will find:

- a scripture reflection based on the Sunday readings
- some questions just to think about or discuss with others
- the true story of someone who has been a witness to the different values of the Gospel
- ideas about some action steps you could take
- suggestions for prayer around the Advent candles
- a Christmas carol or song to read, sing, or meditate on

Advent is a time when many churches meet together. For this reason we have indicated the very slight variations between the Anglican and Catholic Lectionaries at the beginning of each session. Free Church Christians will find that these readings also agree with their Lectionary.

Our wish is that this book will help to renew hope and stimulate energy so that all of us can pray and work together to make 'Thy kingdom come' come true.

VALERIE FLESSATI
BRUCE KENT

SoF 1595 what child is this
1931 Joy has dawned upon the world.

First week of Advent

Pick up your trowel

Isaiah 2:1-5
Psalm 121
Romans 13:11-14
Common Worship: Matthew 24:36-44
Catholic Lectionary: Matthew 24:37-44

If you are a gardener, however part-time or unprofessional, Advent is the time for you. You will know better than most what it is all about.

Gardens are not like museums where everything is labelled and stays on its shelf. Gardens are alive. Even in what the carol calls 'the bleak midwinter' there is hope for the future. The earth is not dead. It is alive and growing even if the growth is unseen.

The good gardener is there to help that growth come to the beauty of grass, flowers, berries and bushes. Perhaps radishes and courgettes as well.

In the first reading today Isaiah stresses that future hope. 'In days to come' (Isaiah 2:2) are the words he uses. What will happen then? All the nations will come together in peace and common worship. A new kingdom will have arrived. Swords will be turned into ploughshares. In God's kingdom we will study war no more.

St Paul, writing to the Romans, clearly thought that the coming of the new kingdom was just around the corner. Even perhaps in his lifetime. But gardeners cannot rush things.

St Matthew in his gospel reminds us that 'The Son of Man is coming at an unexpected hour' (Matthew 24:44). The history of Christianity, on the other hand, is dotted with moments when people thought that they knew exactly when Christ would come again. Time and again they were wrong.

Gardeners do not make such mistakes. Who can tell when or where the first daffodil will show its head? The task of the gardener is to get the garden ready with a lot of hard work. In Advent we are not deckchair gardeners but sleeves-rolled-up gardeners, compost-ready gardeners, fork-in-hand gardeners.

All gardeners have one thing in common. The hard work is not done just for the sake of it. It is done because they have an idea in their heads of how beautiful the garden is going to look, full of flowers and healthy vegetables. They spend time eagerly picturing how things could be, looking at seed catalogues, imagining and planning. Not everything is predictable, but there is a sure hope that it *will* be beautiful if they cooperate with the Creator.

That's an Advent idea too. The poetry of Isaiah nourishes our vision of what God's reign might look like. In Advent we can take time to let our minds dwell on those images of peace and justice and see how they could be applied here and now. We are waiting and working because we have a firm hope in the promise of God's kingdom. Our work helps to bring his plan for the world into being, to help make those dreams come true. We have been promised they will come true one day.

Like the bulb below the earth waiting for the early spring warmth, alive but still not seen, the kingdom of God is growing now in every work of love, justice and compassion we undertake. Advent is a time of hope. But of getting ourselves better prepared too.

Reflection points

- How could you make some time this Advent to learn more about God's ways and about how you could 'walk in his paths' (Isaiah 2:3)?

Cards to take away

- Are you hopeful about the future for yourself, your family and the world? What is your vision of good things ahead that enables you to keep working for it day after day?
- How could you cooperate with God the Creator to bring about a world where 'nation shall not lift up sword against nation' (Isaiah 2:4)?

Witness to reconciliation

Pope John Paul II saw peacemaking as an urgent task for everyone, not just for those, like himself, who have the ear of the world's political leaders. He called on everyone to make 'gestures of peace' – and he practised what he preached. The first pope to visit all continents, his trademark gesture of kissing the ground when he got off the plane symbolised the unity of the world and the preciousness of every part of it.

John Paul II understood the power of such symbolic gestures which could speak louder than words. Gestures can reach across barriers, dispel suspicion, and offer healing and reconciliation.

He gave a personal example of reconciliation, most especially by forgiving Mehmet Ali Agca, the man who nearly killed him in 1981, and by visiting him in prison.

He invited leaders of the world's faiths to Assisi in 1986, where they affirmed their united commitment to the work of peacemaking. This spoke volumes to people across the globe sickened by the divisive role of religion in conflicts.

During his pontificate John Paul II also initiated a series of unprecedented apologies on behalf of the Church for the sins of history. For example, visiting Senegal, he begged pardon for the sins which had reduced so many Africans to slavery. And, in a solemn ceremony to mark the millennium, the Pope asked forgiveness for sins committed by Christians against the Jewish people.

Time and again, in places associated with the worst deeds of humanity, the Pope inspired hope and determination for constructive change.

He developed his idea for 'gestures of peace' in several messages for the World Day of Peace each January. This is what he said in 2003:

> In the end, peace is not essentially about structures but about people. Certain structures and mechanisms of peace – juridical, political, economic – are of course necessary and do exist, but they have been derived from nothing other than the accumulated wisdom and experience of innumerable gestures of peace made by men and women throughout history who have kept hope and have not given in to discouragement.
>
> Gestures of peace spring from the lives of people who foster peace first of all in their own hearts. They are the work of the heart and of reason in those who are peacemakers (cf. Matthew 5:9). Gestures of peace are possible when people appreciate fully the community dimension of their lives, so that they grasp the meaning and consequences of events in their own communities and in the world. Gestures of peace create a tradition and a culture of peace.
>
> *Pope John Paul II, World Day of Peace 2003*
> *© Vatican Publishing House*

This first week of Advent . . .

- Be part of creating the peace tradition yourself. Practise making some gestures of peace and pass them on. Reach across a barrier to offer a smile, a handshake, a kind word, an apology, a visit . . . Start a conversation with someone very different from yourself. Make contact with people at a local mosque, synagogue or temple.
- Do some research and then write to your MP about an issue where human life and dignity need defending: modern-day

slavery/human trafficking; trade justice/debt cancellation; abortion/care of the elderly and terminally ill; nuclear weapons/ the arms trade; the treatment of prisoners/imprisonment without trial.

- Collect some pictures of people who might be thought of as 'enemies' and include them in your prayers. Let their presence help to stretch your idea of family to include all people. Support a group working with and for those people.
- Write down what you would like to do more of, and less of, in your Christmas arrangements this year. What are all the decorations, cards, presents and festivities for? How do you want to spend your time and with whom? For a fresh take on celebrating Christmas contact Alternativity, c/o Christian Aid, 759 Argyle Street, Glasgow G3 8DS; telephone: 0141 221 4242; website: www.alternativity.org.uk
- Make your own Advent wreath. Fix four candles into a circle of wire or green oasis foam from a florist, or simply into candle-holders on a small tray. Decorate this with evergreen foliage from the garden, some holly and ivy perhaps, a few red berries, pine cones, ribbon, or whatever else is to hand. Light one candle on the first Sunday of Advent, two on the second and so on. Make this a special little ceremony with your family, perhaps before tea or supper.

Prayers round the Advent candle

We light this Advent candle
as we wait in joyful hope
for the coming of Christ our light.

(Light the first candle.)

Scripture: Isaiah 2:3

Come, let us go up to the mountain of the Lord,
to the house of the God of Jacob;
that he may teach us his ways
and that we may walk in his paths.

Petitions

May we understand more this Advent about God's dream for the human family and what our own role should be in making that dream come true . . .

Make us people of peace, bringers of reconciliation and healing to those we meet, builders of trust and confidence in our world . . .

We pray for the people of Iraq, Iran and their neighbours, and for all who are threatened with war. May they be kept safe from harm . . .

We pray for all those with whom we need to be reconciled, in our family, friendships, community, nation, or world . . . Ask for the grace to forgive any past wrongs, and to be forgiven too . . .

We pray that the great religions of the world may be agents of peace and understanding . . .

Add your own petitions.

Prayer: A Cry for Peace

To you, Creator of nature and humanity, of truth and beauty,
I pray:

Hear my voice,
for it is the voice of the victims of wars and violence
among individuals and nations.

Hear my voice,
for it is the voice of all children who suffer
and will suffer when people put their faith in weapons and war.

Hear my voice,
when I beg you to instil into the hearts of all human beings
the wisdom of peace, the strength of justice
and the joy of fellowship.

Hear my voice, for I speak for the multitudes in every country
and every period of history
who do not want war and are ready to walk the road of peace.

Hear my voice, and grant insight and strength
so that we may always respond to hatred with love,
to injustice with a total dedication to justice,
to need with sharing of self, to war with peace.

O God, hear my voice,
and grant unto the world your everlasting peace.

Pope John Paul II

Song: The people who stumbled in darkness

Roger Ruston, based on Isaiah 9:2-7 — Traditional Irish melody

THE FOGGY DEW Irregular

2. For every plane and every bomb
and every boot and gun,
and every blood-stained battle-dress
will be burned in the fire to come.
A child is born who will put an end
to the killing and the grief.
The Holy One has given a Son,
our brother, our Prince of Peace.

3. His justice and care will be everywhere
and all terror and lies will cease.
The poor and the lame will praise his name
in truthfulness and peace.
And the nations will rise and learn to prize
the laws that he will teach.
And the world will rejoice
when they hear his voice
and the gospel that we preach.

Second week of Advent

Put on some new glasses

Isaiah 11:1-10
Psalm 71
Common Worship: Romans 15:4-13
Catholic Lectionary: Romans 15:4-9
Matthew 3:1-12

It was only when I got new long-range glasses recently that I realised I had been reaching the point when I was in danger of not being able to read road signs in time. Getting road signs wrong can easily get you lost or, worse, into an accident and then a police station and court.

Advent is all about looking for the right signs and reading them properly. Isaiah gives us a list of quite impossible signs of the kingdom of the future. Lions start to eat straw, snakes stop biting and wolves go to sleep beside lambs. All quite incredible. Moreover, a new shoot is to appear on the root of Jesse – in other words in the line of King David. There will be a connection with the past, but a new world of very different standards and values is on its way. New criteria and measures will be applied because God judges not by appearances or hearsay but by justice. In this reversal of human values, God takes the side of the poor.

Race and pedigree meant everything to people at the time of Jesus, just as they mean so much today. The chosen people were convinced that they were very special. We all know the feeling. Pushed to extremes, that kind of thinking leads to violent nationalism, football punch-ups and even racism. Such are certainly not the signs of God's kingdom.

John the Baptist could recognise the insincerity of those who came to him for baptism with this sense of their own superiority, but without repentance in their hearts. They thought it did not matter because they came from the line of Abraham. 'God is able from these stones to raise up children to Abraham' was the Baptist's reply (Matthew 3:9). The sign of true repentance would be a marked difference in their behaviour.

Just as new shoots appear on old wood in unexpected places, the willingness to change and adopt the different standards of the new kingdom is open to everyone. This surprising truth was demonstrated on the day of Pentecost – a day that gave us one of the greatest lessons of our faith. Many peoples, many languages, but all together as children of God. God has no favourites. The Apostle Peter had trouble learning that lesson but he finally came to understand, as we read in the Acts of the Apostles, that 'God shows no partiality' (Acts 10:34).

That is not an easy truth to accept in our everyday life today, at work, school or church. New people and their different customs are not always welcome. The greatest sign of a new world is an openness and love for all, wherever they come from, together with a respect for their equality with us.

Advent offers us an opportunity to put on some new glasses and see things differently. Recognise and reject the old values whereby what matters is where you come from, how big your salary is, and how famous you are.

Look around for and follow the signs of the new kingdom. They are justice, nonviolence and love for all people, especially those on the edges of society. The knowledge of the Lord is going to fill the earth, says Isaiah, and as a consequence there will be a dramatic change in behaviour: we will not hurt or destroy any of God's holy creation.

Perhaps lions will not eat straw and wolves will not make safe bedfellows for lambs. But the revolution in values will be just as astonishing when the kingdom we have been promised is seen in all its glory. This revolution was powerfully forecast by Mary, when she met her cousin Elizabeth and poured out her praise to God in the words we know as the Magnificat. Princes to be pulled down from their thrones, and the rich sent away empty? That is certainly turning the values of this world upside-down.

Reflection points

- What do you see as the connection between our knowledge of God and looking after God's creation? What images of harmony and peace might Isaiah use today?
- What can we learn from Mary's Magnificat about how the values of our culture and world contrast with God's values? Make a list of those that differ (such as the value of human life, money, class and status, success . . .). Where do you find it most difficult to see things through the eyes of the Gospel?
- How could we – and our society – judge less by appearances and more by justice and equity?
- What would it take to transform the violence of our world? More money? Personal conversion? More prayer? More people involved in change? Education? Add your suggestions.

Witness to justice

Ever noticed the people who clean up after us – in our offices, hospitals, banks and cinemas? They're often migrant workers paid a pittance for long hours and sometimes disgusting work. Many get no more than a grudging minimum wage but no pension, holiday or sickness pay. The contracting-out of cleaning services has meant that unscrupulous companies reduce their employees' wages and job security in the competition to provide the cheapest service.

Slowly but surely a campaign is winning justice for this hidden army of essential workers. It was begun by The East London Communities Organisation (TELCO), which is a network of churches, mosques, religious congregations, tenants' associations, schools and trade unions.

Companies at London's prestigious Canary Wharf development were among the first to be challenged to pay cleaners a living wage. Martin was among the cleaners at Canary Wharf who joined in. He knew from the Church's social teaching that workers must be paid a decent wage – enough for a family to live on comfortably. When the Chairman of HSBC, Sir John Bond, refused to discuss low wages despite the bank's soaring profits, Martin took part in a nonviolent blockade of HSBC's busy Oxford Street branch one lunchtime. Some TELCO supporters used the cash machines continuously, and occupied the cashiers with various enquiries, while others picketed outside with placards and leaflets. For an hour almost no 'real' business got done.

Other TELCO tactics have seen cleaners addressing the annual general meeting of companies and embarrassing highly paid executives. One by one the seven big banks based at Canary Wharf gave in, and now pay a 'Living Wage'. Other victories have followed. Cleaners at several London hospitals have seen their pay rise from £4.50 to £7.50 an hour, with sick pay and longer holidays, and Queen Mary University has become the first 'Living Wage Campus', bringing cleaning services back in-house and paying staff a decent rate. An ethical contract has now been signed by the 2012 Olympics Committee ensuring a Living Wage for all staff engaged in preparations for the Olympic Games.

TELCO and its sister organisations in the wider network of London Citizens and the Citizens Organising Foundation have proved that ordinary people, with training and concerted planning, can use their own power for the common good. It's a win-win process. Who was one of TELCO's allies speaking at its tenth anniversary assembly last year? Sir John Bond, former chair of HSBC!

This second week of Advent . . .

- Think about those for whom Christmas is a time of anxiety or sadness because they are lonely, depressed, far away from family, or afraid of the usual arguments and trouble at home. Think of people in your own circle and neighbourhood . . . in this country . . . elsewhere in our world. . . . What could you do to express solidarity with them and make life a bit easier at this time?
- Add some strangers to your Christmas card list. Each year Amnesty International invites us to send a greeting to a prisoner of conscience or to other individuals or groups whose human rights are abused. Get your friends to take part in the Greetings Card Campaign. Details from: Amnesty International, UK Section, The Human Rights Action Centre, 17-25 New Inn Yard, London EC2A 3EA; telephone: 020 7033 1500; website: www.amnesty.org.uk
- Find out from your local branch of the Red Cross whether they need winter clothing for refugees living in your area. If they do, organise a collection of good quality clothes at your church one weekend. Ask for volunteers to help you, and drivers to deliver the bags the next day.
- Write down the ways you could buy less but give generously to family and friends, investing in relationships more than things. For example, by offering to help, decorate, make, repair, teach a skill, share, sew, find, cook or bake, look after, take out, baby-sit, plant, renew, deliver, listen to, organise, play with, write, drive, visit, paint or build . . .
- Allow yourself space in your diary to slow down this Advent and spend some time in prayer and reflection. Why not plan a 'quiet day' in your church, with gentle background music, candles and nativity icons, where people can find a warm, calm and peaceful refuge away from the shopping and stress before Christmas.

Prayers round the Advent candles

We light these Advent candles
as we wait in joyful hope for the coming of Christ our light.

(Light two candles.)

Scripture: Matthew 3:2-3

Repent, for the kingdom of heaven has come near . . .
A voice of one crying out in the wilderness:
Prepare a way of the Lord,
make his paths straight.

Petitions

May Advent be a time that helps us become better followers of the Gospel, more courageous in standing up for justice . . .

We pray for the refugees who have had to leave their homes and families behind . . . and especially for the children frightened and brutalised by the sight and sound of fighting . . .

Open our hearts to welcome and care for all those who come to our country in need . . . but with gifts to bring us too . . .

May God comfort all those in prison, and those who miss them so much at home . . .

Add your own petitions.

Prayer for asylum-seekers

Lord,
no one is a stranger to you
and no one is ever far from your loving care.
In your kindness watch over refugees and asylum seekers,
those separated from their loved ones,
those who are lost,
and those who have been exiled from their homes.
Bring them safely to the place where they long to be,
and help us always to show your kindness
to strangers and those in need.

Adapted from the opening prayer,
Mass for Refugees and Exiles,
© Australian Catholic Social Justice Council

Carol: God bless us and disturb us

vs. 1&3 John L. Bell & Graham Maule
v. 2 & alternative v. 3 adpt., Bernadette Farrell

Traditional English melody

GOD REST YOU MERRY 77 77 86 and Refrain

2. Where people of all nations
long for justice which is true,
where millions of our children
cry for food which is their due,
where weapons still are traded
bringing fortune to the few:

3. To Bethlehem, to Bosnia,
Whitehall and Central Park;*
to where a star is needed,
since the dark is doubly dark;
to where our lives require the Lord
to set on them his mark;

Alternative text for verse 3

3. To Bethlehem, Afghanistan,
Iraq and Camden Town;*
to where a star is needed
in the darkness all around,
to where our lives await a sign
that peace may now be found:

* *Insert a three-syllable place name, for example your town, church or school; however, it's best if the 2nd, 4th and 6th lines rhyme.*

Kieth or Jane,

Third week of Advent

Recognise what's in front of you

Common Worship: Isaiah 35:1-10
Catholic Lectionary: Isaiah 35:1-6, 10
Psalm 145
James 5:7-10
Matthew 11:2-11

There used to be a poster going the rounds in church circles. It showed a slightly confused and pious-looking man standing in a court dock with a stern judge looking down on him. The caption underneath just said, 'If being a Christian was a crime, would there be enough evidence to convict you?'

This week's readings are all about real evidence. John the Baptist is in prison awaiting his unknown fate. He sends messengers to Jesus to ask him if he is the one they have been told to expect.

That is rather odd, since John was the one who baptised Jesus. He must have heard the voice from heaven saying, 'This is my Son, the Beloved, with whom I am well pleased' (Matthew 3:17). But this seeming contradiction is only odd if we think of the Gospels as a day-by-day diary history, and not a great mix-up of memory and tradition written down years after the events occurred.

Jesus answers John's messengers and the bystanders who would have gathered in crowds in rather different ways.

To the messengers he just says, 'Look around you. Your search is over. The day of God's justice has arrived, here and now. The one promised by Isaiah has to be me. In my life and work you are seeing the amazing signs that were predicted. Look at what is happening to the blind, the lame, the lepers and the poor. That's just what was promised and, in my work, these miracles are already in front of you, turning human expectations upside down and bringing about astonishing changes.'

When the messengers are starting to go he turns to the bystanders to tell them about John. John must have been an object of great curiosity. Some people had even been out into the desert to have a look at him.

It wasn't a wind-blown reed they went out to see. Plenty of those in deserts. Nor a wealthy person in fine clothes. Not many of those in deserts. They went out looking for a prophet and Jesus tells them that, in John, that is just what they found. Repentance and new ways of living are part of the package.

Go back to the poster. In Advent we are all in the dock. What is the practical evidence of our Christian life? Parish pilgrimages and prayer groups? The debt on the hall paid off? A thriving youth club and lots of people at church? Good music and liturgy? All these are fine in their own way.

But Jesus expects more radical evidence that we have recognised the signs and adopted his priorities and example. Care for prisoners, the poor, the sick and the strangers living around us. A challenge to our so unequal national and global society. A positive rejection of the values of money and status. Peacemaking locally and between nations. A willingness to stand up to the Caesar of our day and to be unpopular – as we will be when we challenge the norms of power, moneymaking, injustice and violence of our world.

St James also tells us to be patient and strong. This is not a contradiction. We know we are engaged in a difficult struggle as we live with feet firmly on the earth, while our hopes and best efforts are directed to helping God's reign come about. The signs of that kingdom may be in front of us, but it is also a slow process and completion is somewhere in the future.

Being in the dock is an uncomfortable place to be but Advent is an uncomfortable time of the year. Is there enough evidence on which to convict us?

Reflection points

- Do you feel you are an admirer or a disciple of Jesus? What difference does this make in your life?
- What 'Good News' would the poor want to hear?
- Is your church community involved in any struggles for human dignity, the environment or peace? If not, should it be? What might be your role?

Witness against violence

The phone rings and 80-year-old Mary writes down an address in inner-city Milwaukee. It means another violent death has occurred. Another prayer vigil is planned.

Early next morning she gets the bus and finds the house. Some of her group have already gathered on the pavement. They started as strangers but over time have become friends: old, young, ordinary people of all races and different faiths.

Sometimes only a few can make it, but Sister Rose, the group's coordinator, is always there. She follows up on each newspaper report of someone being killed in the city. She contacts the grieving family to offer sympathy, to tell them that the group will remember and pray for their murdered relation, and to invite them to take part. Sometimes they do. Then Sister Rose activates the telephone tree that reaches more than 50 regular vigilers and has brought Mary here this morning.

Close to the murder site the circle forms. Someone tells the neighbours why they have come and invites them to join in. Then they offer spontaneous prayers, songs and readings. They always remember the victims, their families and friends, those who commit such acts of violence and their families too. They pray for themselves and their fellow citizens, that together they will find ways to end the plague of violence. The vigil ends with hugs of support for family members, the victim's friends and for each other. There are often moments of raw emotion and truth-telling, of tears, faith and forgiveness.

Over 1000 vigils have taken place since 1993 when Milwaukee's religious leaders decided that a there should be a spiritual response to the drive-by shooting of a 12-year-old. The prayer vigils have been compared to a 'wailing wall' as people cry out to God in their desolation and suffering. By their simple presence the vigilers recognise that every life and every death matters. They bear witness, as Mary puts it, to connectedness. 'I am grateful to be part of this solidarity movement; to be present to the hidden Christ among the poor, to be there when Christ is humiliated, scarred and ignored; to give and to receive love.'

This third week of Advent . . .

- Notice the stories in your local newspaper about people who have suffered violence in your area – and especially if this results from a 'hate crime' against those of a particular race or religion. Remember the victims and the perpetrators in your prayers. Is there anything more you could do, maybe with others from your church, to express your compassion for the victims but also to prevent such crimes?
- Look through the listings for this week's television programmes. How many are using war and violence as entertainment? Give them up for Advent.
- This Christmas what toys and games are you planning to give to the children you know? Avoid war toys and choose some which will develop their creativity and teamwork. Think of other gifts which they will remember for ever: a mystery outing, concert or sports activity.

- Make a commitment to find out more about and support the '*Live*simply' initiative of Christian organisations working for social justice and the progress of all the world's people. More details from *Live*simply Project Coordinator, telephone: 01293 541334; website: www.livesimply.org.uk
- Start doing your bit now to protect the planet: turn down the heating, walk, cycle or take the bus rather than drive, switch off lights and computers when not needed, use less water, see how much refuse you can recycle!

Prayers round the Advent candles

We light these Advent candles
as we wait in joyful hope for the coming of Christ our light.

(Light three candles.)

Scripture: Matthew 11:3-5

'Are you the one who is to come, or are we to wait for another?' Jesus answered them, 'Go and tell John what you hear and see; the blind receive their sight, the lame walk, the lepers are cleansed, the deaf hear, the dead are raised, and the poor have good news brought to them.'

Petitions

We pray for all who have died as victims of violence on the streets . . .
And for those who grieve for them . . .

We pray for social workers, police officers, local leaders and politicians, that God will guide them in building a more inclusive and harmonious community in our towns and cities . . .

Giving thanks for all God's gifts, may we learn to live more simply and share the good things of this earth so that there will be enough for everyone's needs . . .

God bless all children and young people with a bright future of equality in which they can offer their unique gifts for the whole human family . . .

Add your own petitions.

Livesimply prayer

Compassionate and loving God,
you created the world for us all to share,
a world of beauty and plenty.
Create in us a desire to live simply,
so that our lives may reflect your generosity.

Creator God,
you gave us responsibility for the earth,
a world of riches and delight.
Create in us a desire to live sustainably,
so that those who follow after us
may enjoy the fruits of your creation.

God of peace and justice,
you give us the capacity to change,
to bring about a world that mirrors your wisdom.
Create in us a desire to act in solidarity,
so that the pillars of injustice crumble
and those now crushed are set free.

Amen.

Carol: It came upon the midnight clear

Edmund Hamilton Sears (1810-1876) alt. — Traditional English melody

2. Yet with the woes of sin and strife
the world has suffered long;
beneath the angel-strain have rolled
two thousand years of wrong;
and warring humankind hears not
the love-song which they bring:
O hush the noise of mortal strife,
and hear the angels sing!

3. For lo, the days are hastening on,
by prophets seen of old,
when with the ever-circling years
shall come the time foretold,
when the new heaven and earth shall own
the Prince of Peace their King,
and all the world send back the song
which now the angels sing.

Mark WL / Andrew. Leading

Fourth week of Advent

Be the good news you want to hear

Common Worship: Isaiah 7:10-16
Catholic Lectionary: Isaiah 7:10-14
Common Worship: Psalm 80:1-7
Catholic Lectionary: Psalm 23
Romans 1:1-7
Matthew 1:18-25

We have heard a lot about signs and waiting during the past three weeks of Advent. This is the last Sunday before the great events of Christmas. Once more the first reading from Isaiah is about getting a sign – or, to be more accurate, about not wanting one.

Ahaz, who receives an unflattering mention in 2 Kings 16, was not exactly a model of kingship. In fact, he was anything but full of zeal for his God during his 20 years on the throne. God tells Ahaz, at a time of peril for the people, to ask for a sign that God is with them, and the foolish man refuses to do so. But God gives him one anyway: a maiden will be with child.

No wonder that, when the story of Christ's birth was told, St Matthew points us back to remind us of the sign given to Ahaz. So St Joseph, a worried man, was given by an angel the sign he needed. Mary's baby was part of God's plan. Jesus was to be the new Emmanuel.

We all like looking for signs that seem to interpret life's mysteries and offer a bit of 'proof'. Predictions about the future and tales of miraculous events and wonders are always fascinating. They are very popular in all religions and outside religions too. Newspapers all have their astrologers.

The signs of God are not just in extraordinary events. On the contrary, it is in ordinary events that God is most apparent (such as a baby being born). We can be so interested in calamities and TV bad news that we do not notice the wonderful love and concern shown all the time by so many to their neighbours. It is pain and evil that hits the headlines.

The selfless love of parents for children – where did that come from? The devoted care of sons and daughters for frail and even difficult parents – where did that come from?

We hear a lot these days about carbon footprints big and small. God's footprints are so obvious but too often get overlooked. The astonishing beauty and design of the vast world in which we live, with its incredible variety of creatures: no accident surely?

Even in the great mystery of pain and suffering there is evidence of God. Where did that sense of justice, which shocks us when we see innocent suffering, come from? The signs of God are everywhere, in our hearts, as well as all around us.

This is the last week of Advent. Is it all over with the Christmas trees, the carols, Midnight Mass, the presents and the turkey? Not at all. Christmas is only the beginning of what we are waiting for.

In fact, waiting is probably the wrong word because that sounds like people sitting in a railway waiting room, bored and looking at their watches. There is another kind of waiting – as anyone who has had a family wedding will know well – and it means a great deal of activity for everyone.

Advent is a reminder every year and all year that we are people on the move, marching to the sound of a different drum. That is why we ought often to be out of step with the ways of the world of today. We have our eyes on the world of tomorrow – God's kingdom which grows around us all the time with its own set of values. That was the kingship that Jesus claimed when he stood in front of Pilate.

That stress on activity may be why those who chose the readings for this week selected a piece from St Paul's letter to the Romans. Paul was a man with a mission to take the Good News 'among all the Gentiles' (Romans 1:6). If, as Christians, we have no sense of mission, then there is something wrong. Faith in God, visible in Jesus Christ, is not just a weekly habit that takes us to church. It demands not routine habit but a pressing sense of purpose.

We are not spectators but active builders when it comes to the cultivation and growth of the kingdom of God. We can see the signs that God is with us if only we want to look. Every new baby, making itself loudly heard, is also another Emmanuel sign that God has faith in human beings. Another world is possible. Life moves forward with every day that passes towards the promises of God.

Reflection points

- How can we learn (like Joseph) to trust that God is making something good out of our lives and actions in some way that we cannot see?
- Take more notice of the good and hopeful signs of God's presence in the world. What creates awe and wonder in you?
- How can God use you to make things new? What talents, gifts and resources do you have to offer in bringing about God's reign of justice and peace?

Witness to solidarity

'The situation in the Middle East is desperate. It is the cradle of three of the greatest faiths in the world and yet experiences much violence and distrust. It needs members of the international community to stand in solidarity with the people of the region and report on what they see. Now that my own children are independent, I have the opportunity to offer three months of my life to do this.'

That's how Rosemary explained her decision to exchange the security of her home in Derby for the insecurity of Nablus, a city in the Palestinian territories, which has been disfigured by bombed buildings, roadblocks and checkpoints, teargas and gunfire. (Historically, it was also the place where Jesus met the Samaritan woman.)

Rosemary first heard about the World Council of Churches' Ecumenical Accompaniment Programme at a meeting some months earlier. Volunteers were needed, and someone said, 'You've just been made redundant. Why don't you go, Rosemary?' Later, on the train home, Rosemary got chatting to another passenger, who turned out to be a Quaker with a similar interest in justice and peace issues. 'Have you ever thought about volunteering as an Ecumenical Accompanier in Israel/Palestine?' the woman asked. 'That was it!' says Rosemary. 'Two messages from God in one day!'

After the selection process and training with 28 volunteers from eight countries, Rosemary joined a small team in Nablus. Their role was to accompany and support local people, and to observe and report on human rights abuses by any group. They hoped that their presence as 'internationals' would help to reduce tension and violence – for example, at checkpoints, where local people have to queue for hours sometimes before the Israeli soldiers allow them through. One day, in Hebron, Rosemary's job was to accompany children to and from school, to see that they got through the checkpoints and to make sure settlers didn't throw stones at them. Another day she sat in respectful silence and wept with the grieving families of two young boys who had been shot. She listened to numerous stories as neighbours poured out their own experiences of loss.

In another village her team helped local people to harvest their olives.

> 'Two things have added to the usual hard work – the fact that it is Ramadan, and the fact that in many places Israeli settlers threaten and physically abuse the olive farmers. The first means that in spite of the heat and dust the workers are fasting from both food and drink throughout the hours of daylight. The second has led to the Israeli authorities promising to protect the pickers on certain days. This means trying to get the complete harvest in three days rather than the 10 or 12 it usually takes . . . We were not expert olive pickers even at the end of the day, but the families entertained us to a feast to thank us.'

When Rosemary left Nablus she commented:

> 'I have laughed, cried, been scared, threatened, challenged and bored – but mostly I have been struck by how awful life is for the majority of Palestinians for most of the time. One thing for me to be stuck at a checkpoint for an hour or so; I always knew I was going to be OK and at the end of three months would be leaving this situation. Not so for those who go through it all the time and who will be hearing gunfire tonight . . . and tomorrow . . . and the night after . . . If my presence meant even a little, I feel my stay in this extraordinary city has been worth it.'

This fourth week of Advent . . .

- Send a message of hope and peace to the people of Bethlehem via the website of Pax Christi International (www.paxchristi.net/xmas/). These messages are channelled through the Arab Educational Institute and other organisations committed to nonviolence and human rights in the Holy Land.

- Make an exhibition in your church about life in Bethlehem today. Pax Christi can provide ideas and information. Pax Christi, St Joseph's, Watford Way, London NW4 4TY, telephone: 020 8203 4884, website: www.paxchristi.org.uk
- As you watch the news or read the newspapers, notice which stories are given priority. Are they 'good' or 'bad' news? Would you expect different stories to be given more importance in terms of their real impact on the world?
- Choose food and drink that is fairly traded and, as far as possible, locally produced when you are planning your Christmas celebrations. Don't buy more than you need – so no food is wasted. Include plenty of soft drinks – to help everyone drive home safely.
- Take part in some activity that builds up your local community. Go carol singing . . . Invite your neighbours round, especially any newcomers, overseas students, elderly . . . Plan and prepare a parish meal.

Prayers round the Advent candles

We light these Advent candles
as we wait in joyful hope for the coming of Christ our light.

(Light all four candles.)

Scripture: Isaiah 7:14

Therefore the Lord himself
will give you a sign.
Look, the young woman is with child
and shall bear a son,
and shall name him Immanuel.

Petitions

Fill our hearts with compassion this Christmas, and make us people who bring good news to others . . .

We remember especially the residents of Bethlehem, that normal life, security and peace will quickly return to the town of Christ's birth . . .

We pray for the mothers and fathers of Palestine and Israel who have lost children in the conflict . . .

May politicians of good will and generosity soon reach a solution there and may the wounds of history be healed . . .

Help us to be more alert to recognise the signs and messengers who show us God's love in this world . . .

Add your own petitions.

Prayer for the Holy Land

Living Lord, ignite in us a passion for justice
and a yearning to right all wrong.
Strengthen us to work for peace
in the land we call holy:
for peace among Jew, Christian and Muslim,
for reconciliation between communities,
for harmony between faiths.
Inspire us to act with the urgency of your quickening fire,
for blessed are the peacemakers:
they shall be called children of God.

Song: Peace Child

Shirley Erena Murray | Bernadette Farrell

2. Peace Child, to the road and the storm,
to the gun and the bomb you come,
you come through the hate and the hurt,
through the hunger and dirt:
bearing a dream.

3. Peace Child, to the dark and our sleep,
to the conflict we reap, now come,
now come: be your dream born alive,
held in hope, wrapped in love:
God's true shalom.